SUMMARY

The

Lean Startup

Eric Ries

**How Today's Entrepreneurs Use
Continuous Innovation to Create
Radically Successful Businesses**

Rapid-Summary

Feel free to follow us on Facebook & Instagram for more summaries:

Facebook:
https://www.facebook.com/BookSummaries-1060732983986564/?ref=aymt_homepage_panel

Instagram:
https://www.instagram.com/booksummaries/

TABLE OF CONTENTS

INTRODUCTION

The Lean Startup is a book written by Eric Ries. In this book, the author explains that regardless of what may often seem to be true, it is very much possible to build a successful startup company.

This book is a guide for all people who think that starting a business will lead to failure. Many startups do end in a failure, because starting a business always comes with uncertainty and risk. Since not all startup founders are equally informed, some are not educated in good business practices and do not have a clear vision of their business; these are the startups that often truly end in failure.

In this book, the author explains how to make a startup successful. This book will surely be a great read for all those who either seek a way for their startup to succeed or for those who are planning to start a business.

At first glance, it certainly looks like an interesting read, and it is both educational and reader-friendly. Whether it is really possible to have a successful startup and whether or not your startup will be successful is what awaits us in this book.

SUMMARY

PART 1:
HOW TO ACHIEVE A FAILURE

The first chapter of the book starts with Eric Ries description of how he worked for a company that ended in failure. The company believed that their products would be worth millions of dollars. They even adopted a seemingly flawless plan and hired many experts, and developed a good infrastructure. Everything revolved around the expected wave of customers that were supposed to buy the company's products.

But unfortunately, the plan never came to pass. The expected customers never really came to a company. The overall result was that the company had lost millions of dollars, and thus ended in failure.

Despite the entrepreneurship of their founders, many other startups also end up in a failure. Many new products are manufactured, but the bad thing about them is that nobody buys and uses them. And because of this, many startups waste tremendous amounts of money, talent, and energy. The author's Lean Startup method is intended to prevent this problem and to greatly reduce the risk of startup failure.

The next thing the author does is compares launching a rocket ship to driving a car. It is known that before a rocket ship is launched into the outer space, there are numerous calculations that need to be made. Even the smallest error can cause a rocket ship launch to end in disaster. But once all calibrations and calculations are done, the ship can be launched, and it is set to go on its course.

On the other hand, driving a car requires constant calculations and thinking. A driver needs to know how and when to steer, to accelerate, or to brake, depending on the situation. But if the driver takes a wrong turn, that will usually not end up in a catastrophe. A driver will need to simply adjust the wheel and get back on the right track.

Many startups behave like a rocket ship. Then they fail because their business assumptions and calculations turn out to be false. And that is exactly where the secret lies: instead of acting like rocket ships, startups should instead navigate like cars. This means that startups should constantly adjust according to the feedback they get from their customers and the market.

PART 2:
THE CORE OF 'LEAN MANAGEMENT'

The second part of this chapter is about the "core" of "Lean Management." The author explains that the Lean Startup method is based on many of the principles of lean manufacturing. Lean manufacturing is a concept developed by Taichi Ohno and Shigeo Shingo, two men working at Toyota.

What is it all about?

First of all, lean manufacturing is a way to eliminate any kind of waste while at the same time producing high-quality products.

This production uses techniques such as:

- Small batch size,

- Production made "just in time,"

- Inventory control,

- Acceleration of cycle times,

- Identifying activities which aim towards value and those that aim towards waste

After this, the author lists things that go under the startup portfolio, such as creating the vision and concept. He also describes which critical decisions need to be made, such as when a startup should react to a customer feedback and when it should ignore such a feedback.

Through all these activities, the author also talks about how a startup makes decisions and defines it framework, which is used to help organize these activities.

The first thing that a startup should have is vision.

Vision is the "foundation" of a startup. It is the main reason why a startup actually exists and the ultimate goal of a startup. The most specific thing about the vision is that it rarely (if ever) changes.

The second most important thing about a startup is a strategy.

Through strategy, a startup is actually progressing towards that vision. It usually involves making the business model, creating a product roadmap, and responding to the market and to competitors. Sometimes the strategy will be changed or "adjusted."

The third thing is the product. Product is actually the end goal of the vision and the overall result of the combination of vision and strategy. The specific thing about the product is that it is evolving.

Another thing, which is vital for the success of a startup, is customer or client feedback. Customer feedback is a sign that tells whether the strategy the company is using is good, and whether the company is on the right track or not.

When talking about the methods of the Lead Startup, it may seem that these methods (such as the technique of small batches) are a bit unconventional and thus it may seem that these techniques may not work. But just because some of these techniques seem different and "out of the ordinary" does not mean that they will be less effective.

At the end of this part of the chapter, the author talks about the ultimate goal of a startup. He says that the ultimate goal of the startup should be figuring out (as soon as possible) what the customers want and what the customers are willing to pay for.

Efforts other than this will only lead to a waste of money, energy, and other resources.

PART 3:
THE NEED FOR DEFINING A STARTUP

The next chapter is about defining a startup. According to Ries, a startup is "a human institution, designed to create a new product or service under conditions of extreme uncertainty."

After the definition, the author presents three key parts of the definition. The first part of the definition is that a startup is human institution. This means that a startup is something much more than just an idea, a technological advancement, or a product, because the main focus is on hiring talent and managing teams.

The second part of the definition is that a startup is a product or a service. This means that a startup can be anything and everything that the customers considers valuable.

The third part of the definition is the extreme uncertainty. This uncertainty is closely connected with the fact that when someone decides to create something new (a product or a service) there is huge amount of uncertainty as to whether that product will be recognized, and thus be successful, or not.

Contrary to this definition, a business that is in its early stage and which follows a proven business model is not a startup. The reason why this is not a startup is because if the customers and products are already known, the future can also be forecast pretty much accurately. Here the success largely depends whether the experts will know how to execute the business plan well enough.

When it comes to extreme uncertainty, both customers and the market are undefined, which leads to the fact that the future is totally unpredictable.

After this, the author discusses the Snap Tax Story. Snap Tax is a perfect example of a so-called startup, which occurred within a large company. The reason why Snap Tax was not considered to be a startup is because it was created within another company, Intuit. That company was the largest developer of finance, tax and accounting tools both for individuals and for small companies.

However, despite Intuit's resources, the Snap tax team began with only five people and the entire team was given something that the author calls an "island of freedom." On that island, the team had the chance to experiment as much as they wanted and they were totally free from any form of management interference.

To sum everything up, innovation is something that is usually decentralized and a very unpredictable process, but Snap Tax showed that it can still be done.

PART 4:
HOW TO CULTIVATE
AN INNOVATION WITHIN
A BIG COMPANY

However, the author says, Intuit did not always cultivate innovation. As time had passed, it became more and more visible that Intuit had a big problem. They did not innovate within Turbo Tax, because they had a conservative past. In the past, only one big innovation had been completed annually before the tax season began. As a result of this, Intuit did not receive any sort of meaningful customer feedback until the tax season. When they finally received customer feedback that they could use, they could not do anything to make any changes to the initial product.

But today, things are different.

Nowadays, Intuit manages to test more than five hundred different changes during their tax season, with up to seventy different tests per week.

Thanks to these frequent and fast testing cycles, not only have the products drastically improved, but the entire entrepreneurial culture has also been greatly encouraged.

The overall result of this is that today Intuit generates 50 million USD in revenue from their new products in twelve months. When we look at how things were before and compare them with how things are today, we will see that there is a huge improvement. Before, it took an average of five and a half years for Intuit to develop a successful new product and to reach 50 million USD in revenue.

PART 5:
THE IMPORTANCE OF LEARNING

The next chapter is about learning. In this chapter the author uses the example of IMVU and their mistakes.

IMVU is a social network where customers can create their avatars, which are actually their virtual characters. Thanks to these avatars, customers can chat and thus interact with one another. When IMVU started their business, their initial idea was to integrate IMVU's experience into already existing instant messaging platforms, such as AOL Instant Messenger. They succeeded in doing that by using "add-ons," which allowed people to share their IMVU experiences with their friends, thus spreading IMVU through the instant messaging network.

It took six months for Ries and his team to work on that add-on. In order to meet the deadline, IMVU had to cut some things which were meant to be included in the program. Because of this, the program was filled with bugs. Even though Ries was tempted to postpone the launch of the program, he knew that the delay would give them negative feedback and so they launched the product.

After they launched the product, they saw that the customers would not even want to download it. After conversation with the customers, the team found out that most of the customers did not even know what the add-on was for. Many customers did not want to invite their friends to IMVU, because many customers were teenagers who did not want to get involved in something that did not look interesting enough. Before they would invite their friends, they wanted to try the product on their own. To deal with this issue, the team created something that they called "single player mode." With this, customers could try out the product alone, but, of course, the use of single player mode was low, because nobody wanted to talk to themselves.

Another step, which was really a desperate measure, was the creation of Chat Now, an app which allowed customers to chat with another randomly connected customer. Finally, the feedback was positive, because customers had fun using Chat Now.

However, when the IMVU team suggested adding these new customers to their AOL messenger list, the feedback was once again negative. The reason for this is that the customers wanted a new messaging program, which would be separate from their already existing IMVU messaging program.

The team assumed that nobody would want another instant messaging network, but this assumption was wrong. Because of that, the team had created one big waste: they made a product that nobody wanted. After all this, what the author wanted to know was why the learning process takes so long and whether some things could have been prevented if they had learned some things faster.

PART 6:
VALIDATE THE LEARNING PROCESS

When people fail in doing something, many people say something like "at least we learned something." But, even though that may be true, a failure, especially in business, is also huge waste of money, resources and effort. But, in order for a startup to succeed, certain things must be learned. A startup needs to know what exactly the customers want and how to give them that.

One way a startup can know whether it is making progress or making things right is by using something that the author calls validated learning. According to Ries, validating learning consists of two ideas:

1. Scientific methods for measuring results and testing hypotheses with key metrics

2. Constant focus on how to reduce waste

That is why startups should run constant and frequent experiments in order to test their hypotheses about their customers and their products. Also, startups should identify key metrics for measuring whether their hypotheses were correct or not.

In lean manufacturing, value is defined as "providing benefit to the customer, while everything else is a waste." The main problem here is that it is hard to determine what a customer may find valuable. That is why the main goal is discovering what the customer values.

PART 7:
ZERO TRANSACTIONS VERSUS
LITTLE TRANSACTIONS

In this part of the chapter, the author explains that, even though it is a paradox, it is still easier to build a team with no transactions than it is with only small transactions available.

The reason for this is while no numbers "invoke" dreams and possibilities, small number invoke fear that these big numbers will never happen. This creates the temptation that the collecting of market feedback should be delayed, but that is also not a good choice, because there are big consequences of delaying feedback. These include wasted work and, of course, creating something that nobody wants.

With validated learning, we actually battle this inclination, because we use data to prove that regardless of everything, the real progress is still being made, despite the fact that the numbers are small.

That is why startups should focus their efforts on real progress and resist the temptation to use vanity metrics (metrics that look better than they are but still do not matter). This way, startups will avoid the "success theater" – an appearance of success, when in reality there is none.

PART 8:
ARE EXPERIMENTS BETTER THAN RESEARCH?

The answer on this question is that they are. In this chapter we will see four main reasons why experiments are better than research.

In order for a startup to learn what the customer needs and wants, many startups do the same thing: they study their markets, and they do all kind of surveys and focus groups.

But according to Ries, there are four reasons why experiments can be as good as, if not better than, research.

The first reason is that many times, market studies and surveys are inaccurate. This means that many customers either do not know what they want or do not know how to say what they want. If we use experiments, we will see what the customers actually want and not what they think that they want.

The second is that lean startup experiments are quick and cheap.

The third is that all sorts of different kinds of feedback from many customers are equally valuable. By experimenting, what a startup does is it actually interacts directly with the real customers, thus learning what their real needs are.

The fourth reason why experiments are a better solution than research is that the experiment is the first product. This means that a successful experiment can be a prototype of a product and something that will attract early customers. Then when a product is ready for launch, it will already have established customers and supporters.

Also, for every startup to succeed, a validation of two types of hypotheses is crucial:

1. Value hypothesis, which explains whether a product or a service will deliver value to customers

2. Growth hypothesis, which determines how a product or a service will spread and grow

But for an experiment to be successful, there are three steps which need to be followed. Preparation is the first step. During the preparation process, a startup should articulate its value and growth hypothesis. Know that if a failure is not an option, then it is not an experiment. The second thing to do is test. Tests should be created and run as quickly and cheaply as possible. The third and the final thing to do before doing an experiment is measure. By measuring, the author means the collection of both data and customer feedback. After doing this, we will be able to see if the results make the hypothesis valid or invalid.

The book summary ends here.

ANALYSIS

The book *Lean Startup*, written by Eric Ries, is a brilliant book about startups and their ups and downs. In his book, the author very thoroughly explains why some startups end up in a failure, while others succeed.

The Lean Startup opens slowly, with the author's introduction into the business and why some startups so easily fail. Things that are immediately seen from the beginning of the book are that the author tries to explain everything that he knows about startups and how the job is supposed to be done. The book is divided into several chapters and each chapter deals with one topic. When we put all the segments together, we see a perfect guidebook for all start up beginners and for those who are uncertain about certain things regarding their business.

One thing that most readers and entrepreneurs will find useful is how the author comprehends the overall concept of a startup, and knows that, if "used" correctly, it will benefit many people. Also, if a startup does not have its core foundations, vision, strategy, and product, it will almost always be condemned to failure. What we will find in this book is a guideline for success of a startup. This does not mean that every startup will be a successful one, but by closely following the author's guides and rules, the chances of success become greatly increased.

QUIZ

This quiz is created as a short test of everything that we learned by reading the summary section. The questions are easy to answer and if someone cannot find the answer in the summary section, all the answers can also be found in the "quiz answers" section. So let's continue.

QUESTION 1

"Regardless of many advances in entrepreneurship, many startups end up in a failure."

      TRUE   FALE

QUESTION 2

According to the author, what are two the most important hypothesis for success of a startup?

a) Growth and value hypothesis.

b) Value and determination hypothesis.

c) Growth and failure hypothesis.

d) Growth and success hypothesis.

QUESTION 3

What should always be the ultimate goal of every startup?

a) The price, which every customer is willing to pay for a product and/or service.

b) The most important goal for every startup is to determine what is that a customer wants.

c) The ultimate goal of every startup is its vision and strong determination to beat the competition.

d) None of the above.

QUESTION 4

"All sorts of different _____ from many _____ are equally valuable. By _____, what a startup does is that it actually interacts directly with the real customers, thus learning what their real needs are."

QUESTION 5

"One way a startup can know whether it is making progress or making things right is by something that the author calls _____."

QUESTION 6

"Regardless of Intuit's huge resources, the _____ team began with only five people and the entire team was given something that the author calls _____."

QUESTION 7

What is a vision and why is a vision important when starting a business?

   a) Vision is what a company is based on; vision is a goal that a company strives to accomplish.

   b) Vision is an ability to predict whether a company will be successful in the future.

c) Vision is each company's main goal. Together with a company's strategy, vision creates a product and/or a service.

d) 'a' and 'c'.

QUIZ ANSWERS

QUESTION 1 – TRUE

QUESTION 2 – a

QUESTION 3 – b

QUESTION 4 – "feedbacks, customers, experimenting"

QUESTION 5 – "validated learning"

QUESTION 6 – "Snap tax, an island of freedom"

QUESTION 7 – d

CONCLUSION

The Lean Startup is a book written by Eric Ries. Even though this summary does not contain everything from the book, it still contains enough information for readers to be presented with the author's main idea.

The book opens with explanations of why certain startups end in failure while others do not. The author also explains that if a startup does not have vision, strategy, and a product or service, it will mostly likely fail, sooner or later. The reason for this failure is that if a startup does not have a clear vision and a well-developed strategy or does not know what customers want, it will create a product or service that nobody will want to use.

Another great thing is that the author uses his own experience and with that experience he explains that instead of making mistakes, which many startups do, we should try not to make mistakes. Although many people perceive mistakes and failures as their opportunity to learn something, a failure often brings many bad "side effects." Some of these side effects are that failure usually means the loss of money, effort and resources, all of which can be detrimental in business.

Through most of this book, Ries tries to explain to his readers what his Lean Startup method is all about. He even explains why little transactions are often better than no transactions for a business and why experimenting can be beneficial for a business to blossom and to succeed.

Throughout the entire book, we can read many explanations, definitions and claims where the author tries to explain to his readers that it is possible to succeed and that success is not something purely reserved for those who "had luck."

There are many reasons why people, especially entrepreneurs, should read this book. Rich with practical advice on the author's new method which greatly increases the chances of success, *The Lean Startup* is a book for every entrepreneur and for those who are looking forward to starting a business. As I wrote above, this summary does not contain everything from the book; there is so much information that it would take at least double the number of pages to explain everything.

Regardless of that, I believe that the readers will get the picture of what the author is talking about and that they will find (just like I did) that *The*

Lean Startup is a very interesting, reader-friendly, and inviting read.

Thank You, and more...

Thank you for spending your time to read this book, I hope now you hold a greater knowledge about **Lean Startup**

There are like-minded individuals like you who would like to learn about **Lean Startup,** this information can be useful for them as well. So, I would highly appreciate if you post a good review on amazon kindle where you purchased this book. And to share it in your social media (Facebook, Instagram, etc.)

Not only does it help me make a living, but it helps others obtain this knowledge as well. So I would highly appreciate it!!

www.amazon.com

FURTHER READINGS

If you are interested in other book summaries, feel free to check out the summaries below.

1- Summary – Hillbilly Elegy by Instant-Summary

   https://www.amazon.com/dp/B076Q9VQN5/

2- Summary – Dark Money by Instant-Summary

   https://www.amazon.com/dp/1979452334/

3- Summary – The Gift of Imperfection

   https://www.amazon.com/dp/B0776RSTY9/

4- Summary - All the Light We Cannot See

   by Instant-Summary

   https://www.amazon.com//dp/B07653T57B/

5- Summary – The Obstacle is the Way

by Instant-Summary

https://www.amazon.com/dp/B075PFY8C
P/

*For more books by Instant-Summary, visit:

https://www.amazon.com/s/ref=nb_sb_noss?url
=search-alias=aps&field-keywords=instant-
summary

Made in the USA
Middletown, DE
14 August 2018